# SUNDAY MORNING

# SUNDAY MORNING

GAIL RAMSHAW

ART BY JUDY JARRETT

LTP

LITURGY
TRAINING
PUBLICATIONS

## Acknowledgments

Gail Ramshaw, a scholar of religious language, is associate professor of religion at LaSalle University in Philadelphia.

Judy Jarrett grew up in Indianapolis where she lives now. She paints furniture, bird houses and postcard-size images. Judy created the art for this book using watercolors, color pencils, gouache and ink on paper.

This book was designed by Jill Smith and Mary Bowers. The type was set in Futura and Palatino by the designers, the cover art was created by Judy Jarrett and Jim Mellody-Pizzato.

Copyright © 1993, Archdiocese of Chicago
Liturgy Training Publications
3949 South Racine Avenue
Chicago IL 60609
1-800-933-1800
fax 1-800-933-7094
e-mail orders@ltp.org

19 18 17 16 15    3 4 5 6 7

ISBN 978-1-56854-081-8
PSUNAM

# PREFACE

We gradually introduce our children to the way the church gathers, reads the Bible and worships on the Lord's Day.

Even before they can read, children can learn from us the wonderful words that Christians speak in the church: ancient words like "alleluia" and "amen," simple prayers like "Lord, have mercy."

This book is built upon those words. Each page offers one such word or phrase printed in large letters across the bottom. The book's first word is "Sunday" and it leads us into the gathering church. The book's last words are "Thanks be to God" as we take leave of one another. In between are many more words that form the Christian vocabulary.

Each page has three other parts, all of them rooted in that key word or phrase. First, at the top of the page, is a sentence whose subject is always "we." These sentences, taken together, are all the actions of the liturgy, all the things we Christians do when we worship together on Sunday. So these sentences trace a journey for child and adult to take together. Gradually, the child becomes familiar with the time when "we sing the angels' hymn" or when "we beg God's Spirit to come to us."

The other two elements on each page—the picture and the short paragraph in the middle of the page—go together. The pictures are of stories from the Bible or from the life of the church. Each is filled with dozens of playful details. The paragraph shows how this particular story can be told to the child as a way to talk about one moment within our Sunday worship.

For example, on the following page is a picture that asks us to tell the story of Zacchaeus. Hidden in the picture you will find the scripture reference to Luke 19:1–10 where you can read the whole story. (You should know that almost all the pictures in the book have a citation of a Bible passage hidden somewhere in them.) The paragraph that begins "Christians gather" also can be read with the child. Then talk about the picture and the story and what it is like to gather with the church on Sunday.

These are possible ways to use this book. But sometimes it is enough for this to be a book of wonderful pictures that tell some of our most important stories.

Children grow into the ways we pray and read our scripture and worship. Little by little the words and songs and gestures of the adult community become the words and songs and gestures of the children. We help them to pray by praying. We help them to sing by singing. Along that way, this book may be one help for children to experience the wonder of our God and of what our church does on Sunday.

# We meet on the first day of the week. ◆ ◆ ◆

Christians gather on Sunday morning because Sunday is the day of Christ's rising from the dead. Zacchaeus wanted to see Jesus. Zacchaeus was so short that he had to climb a tree to see over the crowd. Jesus called Zacchaeus to come down and to join him for a meal. Jesus calls us too.

## Sunday

# We are glad to be baptized. ◆ ◆ ◆

First we remember our baptism. We may cross ourselves with water from the font, or confess our sins and receive God's forgiveness. The church is our ark. Like Noah's family and all the animals, we are safe. The waters of baptism have brought us to the rainbow of God's love.

## In the name of the Father and of the Son and of the Holy Spirit.

# We ask God to smile on us. ◆ ◆ ◆

**W**e are all in need of life from God. Ten people sick with leprosy begged Jesus to heal them, and he did. We too pray that Jesus will show us mercy. And Jesus does.

## Lord, have mercy.

LUKE 17: 11-19

# We sing a song of praise. ◆ ◆ ◆

We join in a song to praise the glory of God.

Miriam and the women danced together after God had

saved them from their enemies.

Today we can clap our hands in joy.

## Glory to God!

EXODUS 15: 20-21

**We pray for ourselves and say Amen.** ◆ ◆ ◆

**I**n a short prayer, we ask God to give us what we need. The people of Israel believed that if they trusted and obeyed God, the walls of Jericho would tumble down.

**O God, Amen.**

JOSHUA 6:1-22

# We hear of God's care for the Hebrew people. ◆ ◆ ◆

**W**e listen to a reading from the

Hebrew Bible. The people of Israel

gathered at a mountain called

Sinai. Moses delivered to them stone tablets

with God's commands written on them. We are

glad that God speaks to us in our world.

## Genesis   Exodus   Ruth   Isaiah

# We sing an old Jewish song. ◆ ◆ ◆

**W**e join together in a psalm, one of the hymns of the Jewish people. The shepherd boy David played the harp as he made up songs to God. We sing to God now and ask God to save us from all evil.

## Save us, O God.

# We hear of God's grace to the first Christians. ◆ ◆ ◆

We listen to a letter written by one of the first Christian teachers. When the Christians met on Sundays in someone's house to share the holy meal, they read Paul's letters aloud. In these same words, God speaks to our church this Sunday.

## Romans    Corinthians    Galatians

# We sing alleluia in praise of Christ— but not during Lent! • • •

We sing an ancient Hebrew word that means "Praise to the LORD." The people of Israel shouted "Alleluia" as they made pilgrimages to the temple to worship God. As we prepare to hear the gospel, we join them in singing praise to God.

## Alleluia!

I KINGS 8

# We stand to hear the good news of Jesus. ◆ ◆ ◆

We listen to a story about Jesus.

The story is taken from one of the four gospel

books. In Jesus, God came to live with us on earth. We

honor Jesus by standing to listen and to respond.

# Matthew  Mark  Luke  John

# The good news comes to us. ◆ ◆ ◆

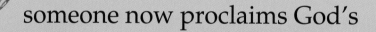

The women at the tomb were the first to announce

to the world that Jesus had won the victory over

death. Following the example of these women,

someone now proclaims God's

good news especially to us.

## Sisters and brothers!

# With all the saints, we believe this.

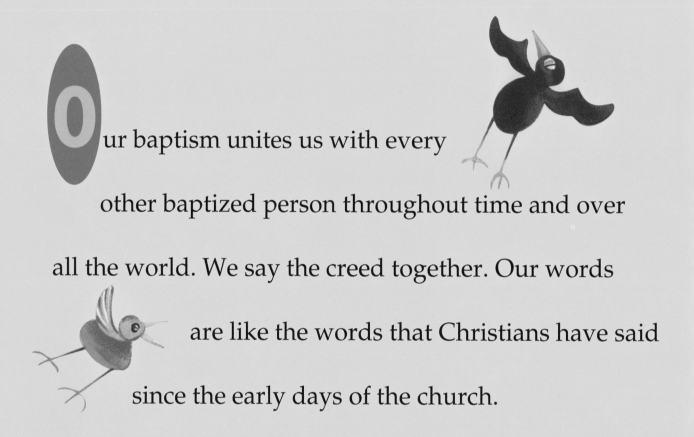

Our baptism unites us with every other baptized person throughout time and over all the world. We say the creed together. Our words are like the words that Christians have said since the early days of the church.

# I believe.   We believe.

# We pray for everyone in the world. ◆ ◆ ◆

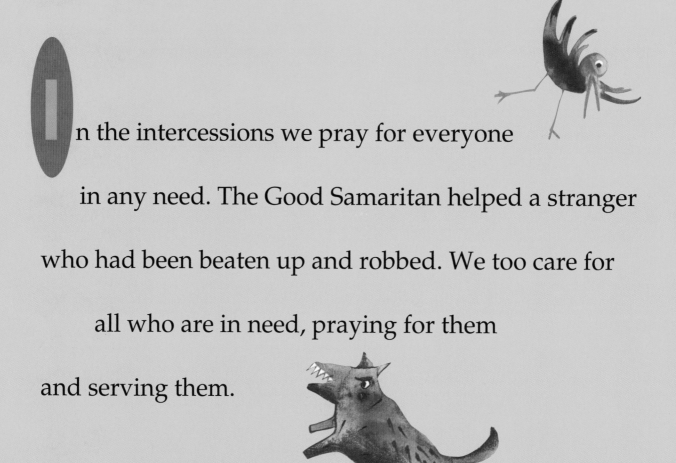

In the intercessions we pray for everyone in any need. The Good Samaritan helped a stranger who had been beaten up and robbed. We too care for all who are in need, praying for them and serving them.

**for the church**  **for the world**
**for the poor**  **for the sick**

# We give our money to others; we bring bread and wine to the table.

**W**e are like the child who gave five barley loaves and two fish. We bring to God our gifts of money, bread and wine. Jesus fed five thousand people with this child's lunch, and there were twelve baskets of leftovers. With our small gifts God does wonderful things.

## Blessed are you.

# We give thanks for all of God's love. ◆ ◆ ◆

We praise God for creation and for mother earth, for centuries of mercy and for the life of Jesus. Every year the families of Israel tell the stories of salvation as they share the passover meal. We also praise God at a meal.

## Lift up your hearts!

EXODUS 12:1-13

# We sing the angels' hymn. ◆ ◆ ◆

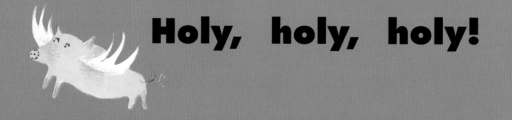

**N**ot only humans praise God. The Bible says that

God is praised by all the animals, and the rain, and the

trees, and nine

different kinds of angels, who don't look

at all like us. We sing the angels' chorus with all heaven

and earth as we bow before the holy God.

## Holy, holy, holy!

# We beg God's Spirit to come to us. ◆ ◆ ◆

**W**e pray that the Spirit of God will

come upon us and upon the wine and bread. On the

day of Pentecost, the disciples saw fire over

their heads. We also are kindled to a new life by

the Spirit of Christ.

## Send your Spirit.

# We pray as Jesus did. ◆ ◆ ◆

**J**esus taught us: If you live as God's children, it is like planting a tiny seed. The seed grows into a tree so big that the birds can build nests in it. We pray for life to be that good for all God's children. We pray the prayer that Jesus taught us.

## Your kingdom come.

**We are blessed at the table. We eat the holy meal. We are the body of Christ.** ◆ ◆ ◆

**W**hen he was a very old man, John had a vision of this meal as a heavenly wedding feast with the Lamb of God on a throne, a tree with twelve kinds of fruit, all the dead come back to life, and no more sorrow or tears. Our meal on Sunday morning is part of that great wedding feast.

**Take, eat.  Take, drink.**

# Once again God's peace comes to us. ◆ ◆ ◆

Over and over on Sunday we are offered the peace of the Lord. In the greeting of peace, we have extended that peace to each other. The disciples who gathered on Easter day were surprised to find Christ there blessing them. Christ comes also to us, embracing us with peace.

# Go in peace.

**We leave in joy and love; we will come back next Sunday morning.**

The shepherds at the stable on Christmas night saw the love of God in the baby Jesus. We too have seen the love of God. Like the shepherds, we go home praising God and loving one another. We can come back together next Sunday to give thanks to God again.

**Thanks be to God.**

*Scripture passages for the illustrations:*

| | |
|---|---|
| **Sunday** | Luke 19:1–5 |
| **In the name...** | Genesis 6:11—9:17 |
| **Lord, have mercy.** | Luke 17:11–19 |
| **Glory to God!** | Exodus 15:20–21 |
| **O God, Amen.** | Joshua 6:1–21 |
| **Genesis...** | Exodus 19:16–25, Exodus 34 |
| **Save us, O God.** | 1 Samuel 16:14–23, Psalm 144:9–10 |
| **Romans...** | Romans 16, Phillipians 1 |
| **Alleluia!** | 1 Kings 8 |
| **Matthew...** | Various gospel stories. |
| **Sisters and...** | Luke 24:1–10 |
| **I believe.** | Holy people. See Ephesians 4:4–6. |
| **For the church...** | Luke 10:29–37 |
| **Blessed are you.** | John 6:1–13 |
| **Lift up...** | Exodus 12:1–13 |
| **Holy, holy, holy!** | Revelation 4:4–8; 5:11–14 |
| **Send your Spirit.** | Acts 2:1–4 |
| **Your kingdom come.** | Mark 4:30–32, Ezekiel 31:3–6 |
| **Take, eat.** | Revelation 21:22—22:5 |
| **Go in peace.** | John 20:19–23 |
| **Thanks be to God.** | Luke 2:20 |